Step by Step

The Story of a Baseball Bat

It Starts with Wood

Robin Nelson

Lerner Publications ◆ Minneapolis

Lerner Publications Company
An imprint of Lerner Publishing Group, Inc.
241 First Avenue North
Minneapolis, MN 55401 USA

For reading levels and more information, look up this title at www.lernerbooks.com.

Image credits: Otto Greule Jr/Getty Images, p. 3; Josef Mohyla/E+/Getty Images, p. 5; age fotostock/Alamy Stock Photo, p. 7; Tim Clayton/Corbis/Getty Images, pp. 9, 15, 17, 19, 23 (logos) (stains); Vespasian/Alamy Stock Photo, p. 11; John Ewing/Portland Press Herald/Getty Images, p. 13; Juan DeLeon/Icon Sports Wire/Corbis/Getty Images, p. 21; BananaStock Ltd. royalty free, p. 22; LightFieldStudios/iStock/Getty Images, p. 23 (bat); Rapiphong Kullathamyothin/EyeEm/ Getty Images, p. 23 (logs). Cover: LightFieldStudios/iStock/Getty Images (bat); Rapiphong Kullathamyothin/EyeEm/Getty Images (logs).

Main body text set in Mikado a Medium.
Typeface provided by HVD Fonts.

Editor: Andrea Nelson

Library of Congress Cataloging-in-Publication Data

Names: Nelson, Robin, 1971– author.
Title: The story of a baseball bat : it starts with wood / Robin Nelson.
Description: Minneapolis : Lerner Publications, 2021. | Series: Step by step | Includes bibliographical references and index. | Audience: Ages 4–8 | Audience: Grades K–1 | Summary: "How does a tree become a baseball bat? Photos and straightforward text will take young readers through the process step by step."—Provided by publisher.
Identifiers: LCCN 2019036649 (print) | LCCN 2019036650 (ebook) | ISBN 9781541597716 (lib. bdg.) | ISBN 9781728401058 (eb pdf)
Subjects: LCSH: Baseball bats—Juvenile literature.
Classification: LCC GV879.7 .N4525 2020 (print) | LCC GV879.7 (ebook) | DDC 796.357/26—dc23

LC record available at https://lccn.loc.gov/2019036649
LC ebook record available at https://lccn.loc.gov/2019036650

Manufactured in the United States of America
1-47916-48362-11/25/2019

Baseball is a blast!

How was my bat made?

First, trees are cut into logs.

Then the logs are cut and shaped.

Next, a worker chooses a piece of wood.

A machine
carves the wood.

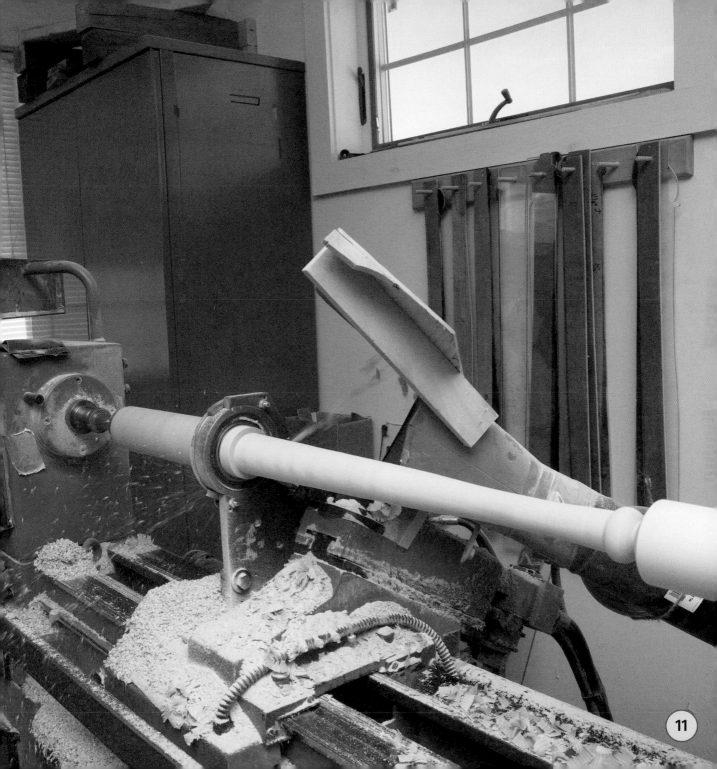

Then the bat is sanded.

13

Next, workers check the bat.

A worker stains
the bat.

Then a machine
adds logos.

TL-TULO-M

PRO SELECT LIMITED 33/30
0627 1498.4

Finally, the bat is shipped.

Batter up!

Read More

Flynn, Brendan. *Baseball Time!* Minneapolis: Lerner Publications, 2017.

Minden, Cecilia. *Tim and His Bat.* Ann Arbor, MI: Cherry Lake, 2018.

Nelson, Robin. *Baseball Is Fun!* Minneapolis: Lerner Publications, 2014.

Index

Picture Glossary

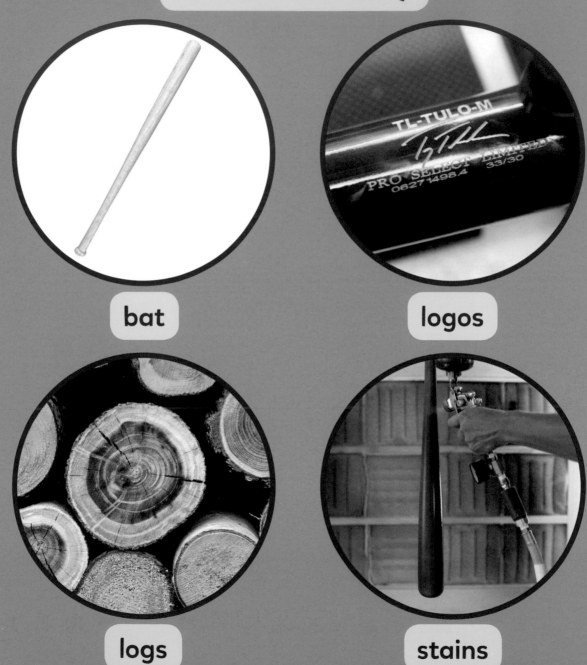

bat

logos

logs

stains